GREAT Songs from WB MOVIES

MW00563089

Editor: Tony Esposito
Creative Consultant Alan Warner
Special thanks to Pat Warner

ISBN 0-89724-580-6

CONTENTS

INTRODUCTION

Film music has come a long way since sound was first introduced back in the late1920's. It was Warner Bros. who officially launched the genre on a cold New York evening in October 1927 when "The Jazz Singer" was given its world premiere. The film was basically a silent drama with a synchronized back-ground score, but with some inserted dialogue and musical sequences, it started a revolution. The electrifying performances by Al Jolson in what was billed as "Warner Bros.' supreme triumph" were more than enough evidence to back-up Jolson's on-camera promise: "You ain't heard nothin' yet!"

This giant volume of memorable melodies from almost seventy years of Warner Bros. movies draws on a myriad of sources and represents some of the greatest American songwriters. The unforgettable Busby Berkeley-choreo-graphed musicals of the 1930's are recalled by the Oscar-winning LULLABY OF BROADWAY along with 42ND STREET, SHUFFLE OFF TO BUFFALO, I ONLY HAVE EYES FOR YOU, THE LADY IN RED, REMEMBER MY FORGOTTEN MAN, YOU'RE GETTING TO BE A HABIT WITH ME, WITH PLENTY OF MONEY AND YOU, YOUNG AND HEALTHY, BY A WATERFALL plus WE'RE IN THE MONEY which almost singlehandedly blew away the cobwebs of Depression and was officially tagged "The Gold Diggers' Song."

A number of the Warner songs have been featured in more than one motion picture; for instance, TOO MARVELOUS FOR WORDS was introduced in the 1937 musical "Ready, Willing And Able" and then a decade later, it was utilized sev-eral times in the Humphrey Bogart/Lauren Bacall thriller "Dark Passage." Then there's the bittersweet AM I BLUE which the great Ethel Waters introduced in 1929's "On With The Show" and which re-surfaced in at least two more Warner Bros. Pictures; you may also recall that a certain Miss Streisand revived it in "Funny Lady" at another studio and in another era!

Other highlights from early Warner musicals include I'LL STRING ALONG WITH YOU (sung by Dick Powell to and with Ginger Rogers in "Twenty Million Sweethearts"), JEEPERS CREEPERS (sung by Louis Armstrong to a horse in "Going Places"); REMEMBER ME introduced by Kenny Baker in 1937's "Mr. Dodd Takes The Air" (and revived decades later by Shirley MacLaine in her 1970's song-and-dance revue); SEPTEMBER IN THE RAIN serenaded by operatic tenor

James Melton in "Melody For Two"; BLUES IN THE NIGHT sung by William Gillespie in the movie of the same name; A GAL IN CALICO and A RAINY NIGHT IN RIO, both hits which were introduced in 1946's "The Time, The Place And The Girl"; the title song from HOLLYWOOD CANTEEN sung over the credits by The Andrews Sisters; THEY'RE EITHER TOO YOUNG OR TOO OLD which was Bette Davis' specialty number in "Thank Your Lucky Stars" and LULU'S BACK IN TOWN for which Dick Powell joined forces with The Mills Brothers in "Broadway Gondolier." Also from "Thank Your Lucky Stars," there's Dinah Shore's showstopping THE DREAMER and, from "Hollywood Canteen," you'll discover DON'T FENCE ME IN as performed by Roy Rogers & The Sons Of The Pioneers.

Lest we forget, there's tinseltown's (un)official anthem, HOORAY FOR HOLLYWOOD, which was introduced in the opening reels of "Hollywood Hotel" by Benny Goodman & His Orchestra with vocals by trumpet-playing Johnny 'Scat' Davis and vivacious Frances Langford. And talking of signature songs, we've included two "Looney Tunes" and "Merrie Melodies" favorites: MERRILY WE ROLL ALONG and THE MERRY-GO-ROUND BROKE DOWN.

Doris Day was one of Warner Bros.' major musical stars and she is represented here by the glorious IT'S MAGIC which highlighted her debut movie "Romance On The High Seas" and the Academy-Award winning SECRET LOVE which she sang in the barnstorming box-office hit "Calamity Jane." Al Jolson is similarly represented by three of his beloved routines namely SWANEE (sung in his trademark blackface in the George Gershwin biopic, "Rhapsody In Blue"); the humorous SHE'S A LATIN FROM MANHATTAN and the landmark duet number, ABOUT A QUARTER TO NINE with his then-wife Ruby Keeler in the only movie they made together, "Go Into Your Dance."

As the years sped by and musicals went from strength to strength, we found Frank Sinatra on the courthouse steps proclaiming MY KIND OF TOWN (CHICAGO IS) in "Robin And The 7 Hoods" and more than two decades separated Judy Garland's haunting rendition of THE MAN THAT GOT AWAY in the 1954 "A Star Is Born" and Barbra Streisand's tenderly emotive EVERGREEN from the 1976 re-make.

We have also chosen some memorable songs which were performed on-camera in non-musical pictures including the legendary AS TIME GOES BY which was not written for but became forever identified with "Casablanca" in which Dooley Wilson sang it for Humphrey Bogart and to Ingrid Bergman. There is also MOANIN' LOW, the song which lush Claire Trevor sings in "Key

Largo," hoping to score a drink from gangster Edward G. Robinson, I'M JUST WILD ABOUT HARRY which perky Priscilla Lane delivers in "The Roaring Twenties," THIS TIME THE DREAM'S ON ME which the same Miss Lane sings with the band in "Blues In The Night," YOU MUST HAVE BEEN A BEAUTIFUL BABY which Dick Powell croons to Olivia De Havilland in "Hard To Get," HOW LITTLE WE KNOW which both Lauren Bacall and Hoagy Carmichael perform in the wartime thriller "To Have And Have Not," the prophetic YOU'RE GONNA HEAR FROM ME which is performed by Natalie Wood (and ghosted by Jackie Ward) in "Inside Daisy Clover" through to the Oscar-winning WE MAY NEVER LOVE LIKE THIS AGAIN which Maureen McGovern warbled in the disaster epic, "The Towering Inferno."

You'll even discover THAT'S WHAT FRIENDS ARE FOR which most remember as the song which topped the charts in early '86 sung by Dionne Warwick with Elton John, Gladys Knight & Stevie Wonder; however, it was actually written by Burt Bacharach and Carole Bayer Sager for Rod Stewart to sing on the soundtrack of Ron Howard's 1982 comedy "Night Shift."

Theme songs play an integral role on countless movie soundtracks and our selections include AL DI LA which Emilio Pericoli crooned in "Rome Adventure," ARTHUR'S THEME (BEST THAT YOU CAN DO) which co-author Christopher Cross sang in the first "Arthur" picture in 1981 and, for complete contrast, RIDE AWAY which The Sons Of The Pioneers sing as John Wayne turns and walks away at the end of John Ford's "The Searchers." Another stunning example of the impression that a soundtrack theme can leave was Henry Mancini's off-camera chorus singing the Oscar-winning THE DAYS OF WINE AND ROSES in that memorable film. Just a few months after ARTHUR'S THEME topped the Billboard singles charts, Greek composer and keyboard player Vangelis took his haunting melody from CHARIOTS OF FIRE to #1 across America.

Our parade of movie themes rolls right into the '90s with Michael Jackson's WILL YOU BE THERE from "Free Willy," BEAUTIFUL MARIA OF MY SOUL as performed by The Mambo All-Stars featuring Antonio Banderas in "The Mambo Kings," the glorious I HAVE NOTHING which Whitney Houston sang in the box-office smash and her film debut "The Bodyguard," Bryan Adams' worldwide chart-topper, (EVERYTHING I DO) I DO IT FOR YOU from "Robin Hood: Prince Of Thieves," CLAUDIA'S THEME by Lennie Niehaus from Clint Eastwood's landmark western "Unforgiven" and James Newton Howard's MAIN TITLE from the heart-pounding thriller hit "The Fugitive."

To complete our coverage of movie song sources, you'll find a group of songs which were based on themes from significant motion pictures, though the lyrics were not heard in the movies themselves. For instance, Max Steiner wrote a haunting theme which threads its way through the whole of "Now, Voyager," only to swell up after Bette Davis' famous closing line, "Oh Jerry, don't let's ask for the moon... We have the stars." A lyric was added and the popularity of both the picture and the music propelled Dick Haymes' recording of IT CAN'T BE WRONG to the top of the hit parade in 1943. Other songs of similar origin are included, such as AS LONG AS I LOVE which was based on a Steiner melody from "Saratoga Trunk" and LOVE FOR LOVE, whose origin was one of Erich Wolfgang Korngold's themes from "Escape Me Never." Maestros Steiner and Korngold defined the art of dramatic movie scoring in a series of splendid scores for early Warner pictures and their successors in later years at the studio included such giants of the genre as Dimitri Tiomkin ("The High And The Mighty," "The Sundowners," "Land Of The Pharaohs," "The Old Man And The Sea" and "Giant"), Franz Waxman ("Sayonara"), Leonard Rosenman ("Rebel Without A Cause" and "East Of Eden"), Alex North ("Cheyenne Autumn"), Lalo Schifrin ("The Fox"), Michel Legrand ("Summer Of '42", "The Picasso Summer" and "Best Friends"), John Barry ("Petulia"), Dave Grusin ("The Heart Is A Lonely Hunter"), Johnny Mandel ("An American Dream" and "Harper") Henry Mancini ("Wait Until Dark" and "10") and John Williams ("Superman" and "JFK"). Steiner's final years are also represented by "Band Of Angels," "So Big," "Parrish," "Battle Cry," "The Dark At The Top Of The Stairs" and the often-revived and extremely nostalgic THEME FROM A SUMMER PLACE.

Obviously, we know some of the above dramatic themes by the lyrics which were added in certain cases; for instance, the Love Theme from "Superman" was CAN YOU READ MY MIND, sung by Margot Kidder (aka Lois Lane)... The theme from "Summer Of '42" became equally familiar as THE SUMMER KNOWS, while Norman Jewison's comedy "Best Friends" introduced us to the Oscar-nominated ballad, HOW DO YOU KEEP THE MUSIC PLAYING?

So suspend all reality and join us on a musical journey through the rich past and present of one of Hollywood's greatest motion picture studios. You may even find yourself humming along when you least expect it!

ALAN WARNER
Author, "Who Sang What On The Screen"
Angus & Robertson (UK) 1984

Performed by Ethel Waters in "ON WITH THE SHOW" (1929)

AM I BLUE?

Words by
GRANT CLARKE

Music by
HARRY AKST

11

12

The Show of Shows (1929)

LADY LUCK

Words and Music by
RAY PERKINS

15

The Gold Diggers of Broadway (1929)

KEEPING THE WOLF FROM THE DOOR

Lyrics by
AL DUBIN

Music by
JOE BURKE

In ev - 'ry cho - rus la - dy's life, there
It takes some fine ma - nip - u - la - tion

comes a time of storm and strife, when she re - quires___ mon - e - ta - ry aid.___
to a - void com - plete star - va - tion, on the wa - ges of a sweet cho - rine.___

Is Everybody Happy (1929)

IN THE LAND OF JAZZ

Lyrics by
J. KEIRN BRENNAN

Music by
RAY PERKINS

WHEN YOUR LOVER HAS GONE

Words and Music by
E. A. SWAN

25

Performed by Ruby Keeler & Dick Powell in "42ND STREET" (1933)

FORTY-SECOND STREET

Words by
AL DUBIN

Music by
HARRY WARREN

Performed by Ruby Keeler & Clarence Nordstrum in "42ND STREET" (1933)

SHUFFLE OFF TO BUFFALO

Words by
AL DUBIN

Music by
HARRY WARREN

33

Performed by Bebe Daniels in "42ND STREET" (1933)

YOU'RE GETTING TO BE A HABIT WITH ME

Words by
AL DUBIN

Music by
HARRY WARREN

Performed by Dick Powell in "42ND STREET" (1933)

YOUNG AND HEALTHY

Words by
AL DUBIN

Music by
HARRY WARREN

41

Performed by Joan Blondell in "GOLD DIGGERS OF 1933" (1933)

REMEMBER MY FORGOTTEN MAN

Words by
AL DUBIN

Music by
HARRY WARREN

Performed by Dick Powell & Ruby Keeler in "FOOTLIGHT PARADE" (1933)

BY A WATERFALL

Lyrics by
IRVING KAHAL

Music by
SAMMY FAIN

I ap - pre - ci - ate the sim - ple things, _____ 'cause I'm

aw - f'lly fond of get - ting, love in a na - tu - ral set - ting.

48

Performed by Ginger Rogers in "GOLD DIGGERS OF 1933" (1933)

THE GOLD DIGGER'S SONG
(WE'RE IN THE MONEY)

Words by
AL DUBIN

Music by
HARRY WARREN

Allegro moderato

Gone are my blues, And gone are my tears;

I've got good news To shout in your ears.

The sil - ver dol - lar has re - turned to the fold,___ With

Performed by Dick Powell & Ruby Keeler in "DAMES" (1934)

I ONLY HAVE EYES FOR YOU

Words by
AL DUBIN

Music by
HARRY WARREN

54

REFRAIN

Performed by Dick Powell & Ginger Rogers in "TWENTY MILLION SWEETHEARTS" (1934)

I'LL STRING ALONG WITH YOU

(You May Not Be An Angel, But)

Music by
HARRY WARREN

All my life I wait-ed for an an-gel, ___ But no an-gel ev-er came a-

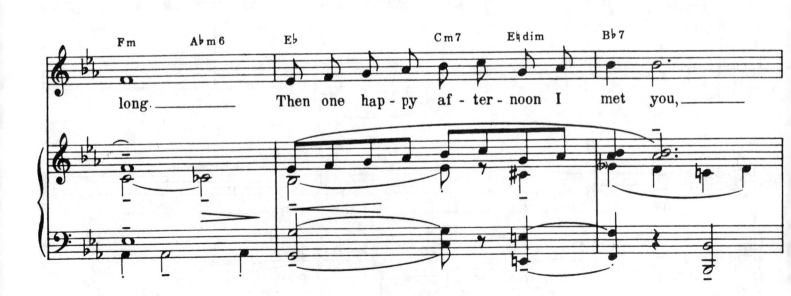

long. ___ Then one hap-py af-ter-noon I met you, ___

57

Performed by Dick Powell in "SHIPMATES FOREVER" (1935)

DON'T GIVE UP THE SHIP

Words by
AL DUBIN

Music by
HARRY WARREN

Gratefully acknowledging valuable suggestions
made by Lt. William Gorden Beecher, Jr., U.S.N.

62

if you have to take a lick - in', car - ry on and

quit your kick - in', don't give up the ship!

Fine

Interlude
Molto marcato

D.S. 𝄋 al Fine

Performed by Al Jolson in "GO INTO YOUR DANCE" (1935)

SHE'S A LATIN FROM MANHATTAN

Lyrics by
AL DUBIN

Music by
HARRY WARREN

Fate sent her to me o - ver the sea from Spain; Ah! She's the one in a

mil - lion _____ for me. _____

Performed by Al Jolson in "GO INTO YOUR DANCE" (1935)

ABOUT A QUARTER TO NINE

Words by
AL DUBIN

Music by
HARRY WARREN

morn-ing un-til twi-light, I don't know I'm a-live,

But I know love be-gins at eight for-ty five.

REFRAIN

The stars _____ are gon-na twin-kle and shine _____

This eve - ning, _____ a-bout a quar-ter to nine. _____

Performed by Winifred Shaw and Judy Canova in "IN CALIENTE" (1935)

THE LADY IN RED (QUERIDA MUJER)

Words by
MORT DIXON

Music by
ALLIE WRUBEL

73

74

Performed by Dick Powell & The Mills Brothers in "BROADWAY GONDOLIER" (1935)

LULU'S BACK IN TOWN

Words by
AL DUBIN

Music by
HARRY WARREN

Moderato

Where's that care-less cham-ber-maid? Where'd she put my ra-zor blade?

She mis-laid it, I'm a-fraid, it's got-ta be foun'.

77

78

MERRILY WE ROLL ALONG

By
EDDIE CANTOR, CHARLIE TOBIAS
and MURRAY MENCHER

Performed by Winifred Shaw & Dick Powell in "THE GOLD DIGGERS OF 1935" (1935)

LULLABY OF BROADWAY

Words by
AL DUBIN

Music by
HARRY WARREN

Come on a-long and lis-ten to the lul-la-by of Broad-way.

The hip hoo-ray and bal-ly-hoo, the lul-la-by of Broad-way.
The hi-dee-hi and boop-a-doo,

The rum-ble of a sub-way train, the rat-tle of the tax-is.
The band be-gins to go to town, and ev-'ry one goes cra-zy.

85

Performed by Dick Powell in "GOLD DIGGERS OF 1937" (1936)

WITH PLENTY OF MONEY AND YOU

(Gold Diggers' Lullaby)

Words by
AL DUBIN

Music by
HARRY WARREN

89

Warner Bros. Cartoons

THE MERRY-GO-ROUND BROKE DOWN

Words and Music by
CLIFF FRIEND
and DAVE FRANKLIN

REFRAIN

lights went low, we both said "Oh" and the mer-ry-go-round went

um-pah-pah, um-pah-pah, um-pah, um-pah, um-pah-pah,

Oh! what fun, a won-der-ful time____

Find - ing love for on - ly a dime,____ THE

93

Performed by Doris Weston in "THE SINGING MARINE" (1937)

I KNOW NOW

Words by
AL DUBIN

Music by
HARRY WARREN

It's not a sign of meek-ness To say you're wrong,

When you dis-cov-er your mis-take,

* *Symbols for Ukulele, Guitar and Banjo*

It does-n't show your weak-ness, It shows you're strong,

When you ad-mit a blun-der that you make; For,

REFRAIN
(Tenderly)

I know now, you're the on-ly one, ____

(Tenderly)
p-mf

I know now, I'm the

Performed by Johnny 'Scat' Davis & Frances Langford with Benny Goodman & His Orchestra
in "HOLLYWOOD HOTEL" (1937)

HOORAY FOR HOLLYWOOD

Words by
JOHNNY MERCER

Music by
RICHARD A. WHITING

100

Performed by James Melton in "MELODY FOR TWO" (1937)

SEPTEMBER IN THE RAIN

Words by
AL DUBIN

Music by
HARRY WARREN

103

105

Performed by Ann Sheridan in "SAN QUENTIN" (1937)

HOW COULD YOU

Words by
AL DUBIN

Music by
HARRY WARREN

* *Symbols for Ukulele, Guitar and Banjo*

109

Performed by Winifred Shaw & Ross Alexander in "READY, WILLING & ABLE" (1937)

TOO MARVELOUS FOR WORDS

Words by
JOHNNY MERCER

Music by
RICHARD A. WHITING

111

112

Performed by Kenny Baker in "MR. DODD TAKES THE AIR" (1937)

REMEMBER ME?

Words by
AL DUBIN

Music by
HARRY WARREN

114

Performed by Louis Armstrong in "GOING PLACES" (1938)

JEEPERS CREEPERS

Words by
JOHNNY MERCER

Music by
HARRY WARREN

Fools for Scandal (1938)

HOW CAN YOU FORGET?

Words by
LORENZ HART

Music by
RICHARD RODGERS

123

Performed by Rudy Vallee & Rosemary Lane in "GOLD DIGGERS IN PARIS" (1938)

DAYDREAMING (All Night Long)

Words by
JOHNNY MERCER

Music by
HARRY WARREN

Daydreaming-3

128

Performed by Dick Powell in "HARD TO GET" (1938)

YOU MUST HAVE BEEN A BEAUTIFUL BABY

Words by
JOHNNY MERCER

Music by
HARRY WARREN

Does your moth-er re-al-ize, The stork de-liv-ered quite a prize, The

day he left you on the fam-'ly tree, Does your dad ap-pre-ci-ate, That

you are mere-ly su-per great, The mir-a-cle of an-y cen-tu-

Dust Be My Destiny (1939)

DUST BE MY DESTINY

Lyrics by
M.K. JEROME and JACK SCHOLL

Music by
MAX STEINER

135

Four Wives (1939)

CLOSE TOGETHER

Lyrics by
KIM GANNON

Music by
MAX STEINER and MAX RABINOWITSCH

CLOSE TO - GETH - ER, we'll spend a

life - time mak - ing dreams come

true. Dar - ling, when it

thun - ders a - bove

I'M JUST WILD ABOUT HARRY

Words and Music by
NOBLE SISSLE and EUBIE BLAKE

Accel. poco-e-poco (2nd time in tempo)

I'm just wild a-bout Har-ry and Har-ry's wild a-bout me.

Moderately fast 2

The heav'n-ly bliss-es of his kiss-es fill me with ec-sta-sy. He's

sweet just like choc-'late can-dy and just like hon-

ALONG THE SANTA FE TRAIL

Music by
WILL GROSZ

Words by
AL DUBIN and EDWINA COOLIDGE

145

Performed by William Gillespie in "BLUES IN THE NIGHT" (1941)

BLUES IN THE NIGHT

(My Mama Done Tol' Me)

Words by
JOHNNY MERCER

Music by
HAROLD ARLEN

147

148

ALL THROUGH THE NIGHT

Words by
JOHNNY MERCER

Music by
ARTHUR SCHWARTZ

When the sun has sunk be-neath the wil - low,

when a star or two tells me an-oth-er day is through

Here's a dream that waits up-on my pil-low,

So I live through the day, Know-ing you'll come my way;

rit.

REFRAIN
(Andante)

ALL THROUGH THE NIGHT you are mine, _____ deep in a

star span-gled dream you are mine, _____

Performed by Priscilla Lane in *"BLUES IN THE NIGHT"* (1941)

THIS TIME THE DREAM'S ON ME

Words by
JOHNNY MERCER

Music by
HAROLD ARLEN

Slowly with expression

Some - where, some - day _____ we'll be close to - geth - er,

wait and see, _____ Oh, by the way,

155

Performed by Al Jolson in "RHAPSODY IN BLUE" (1945)

SWANEE

Words by
IRVING CAESAR

Music by
GEORGE GERSHWIN

158

159

Now Voyager (1942)

IT CAN'T BE WRONG

Words by
KIM GANNON

Music by
MAX STEINER

Performed by Hoagy Carmichael in "TO HAVE AND HAVE NOT" (1944)

BALTIMORE ORIOLE

Words by
PAUL FRANCIS WEBSTER

Music by
HOAGY CARMICHAEL

TOMORROW (WHEN YOU ARE GONE)

Words by
MARGARET KENNEDY

Music by
ERICH WOLFGANG KORNGOLD

When you are gone, the birds will stop their sing - ing;
Say not so! An - oth - er love will cheer you.

Performed by Dooley Wilson in "CASABLANCA" (1942)

AS TIME GOES BY

Words and Music by
HERMAN HUPFELD

Performed by Dinah Shore in "THANK YOUR LUCKY STARS" (1943)

THE DREAMER

Lyrics by
FRANK LOESSER

Music by
ARTHUR SCHWARTZ

173

Performed by Bette Davis in "THANK YOUR LUCKY STARS" (1943)

THEY'RE EITHER TOO YOUNG OR TOO OLD

Words by
FRANK LOESSER

Music by
ARTHUR SCHWARTZ

You marched a-way and left this town as emp-ty as can be, I can't sit un-der the ap-ple tree with an-y-one else but me. For there is no sec-ret lov-er, that the draft board did-n't dis-cov-er.

or too young,_____ So dar-ling, you'll nev-er get stung._____
or too stale,_____ There is no a-vail-a-ble male._____
breath of spring,_____ Or else I'm their last lit-tle fling._____

_____ To-mor-row I'll go hik-ing with that Ea-gle Scout un-less I
I will con-fess to one ro-mance I'm sure you will al-low, He
I eith-er get a fos-sil or an ad-o-les-cent pup, I

get a call from grand-pa for a snap-py game of chess. I'm find-ing it eas-
tries to ser-e-nade me but his voice is chang-ing now. I'm find-ing it eas-
eith-er have to hold him off or have to hold him up. The bat-tle is on,_____

y to stay good as gold.___ They're
y to keep things con-trolled.___ They're eith-er too young_or too old._____ They're
__but the fort-ress will hold.___ They're

Performed by The Andrews Sisters in "HOLLYWOOD CANTEEN" (1944)

HOLLYWOOD CANTEEN

Words by
M.K. JEROME and RAY HEINDORF

Music by
TED KOEHLER

Performed by Kitty Carlisle in "HOLLYWOOD CANTEEN" (1944)

SWEET DREAMS, SWEETHEART

Words by
TED KOEHLER

Music by
M. K. JEROME

Hollywood Canteen (1944)

DON'T FENCE ME IN

Words and Music by
COLE PORTER

Saratoga Trunk (1945)

AS LONG AS I LIVE

Lyrics by
CHARLIE TOBIAS

Music by
MAX STEINER

Performed by Lauren Bacall & Hoagy Carmichael in "TO HAVE AND HAVE NOT" (1944)

HOW LITTLE WE KNOW

Words by
JOHNNY MERCER

Music by
HOAGY CARMICHAEL

187

SOMEDAY I'LL MEET YOU AGAIN

Lyrics by
NED WASHINGTON

Music by
MAX STEINER

189

ONE MORE TOMORROW

By
ERNESTO LECUONA, JOSEF MYROW
and EDDIE DeLANGE

My Reputation (1946)

WHILE YOU'RE AWAY

Lyrics by
STANLEY ADAMS

Music by
MAX STEINER

Performed by Dennis Morgan, Jack Carson, Janis Paige & Martha Vickers in "THE TIME, THE PLACE & THE GIRL" (1946)

A RAINY NIGHT IN RIO

Words by
LEO ROBIN

Music by
ARTHUR SCHWARTZ

195

Performed by Dennis Morgan & Jack Carson in "THE TIME, THE PLACE & THE GIRL" (1946)

A GAL IN CALICO

Words by
LEO ROBIN

Music by
ARTHUR SCHWARTZ

Performed by Dennis Morgan, Martha Vickers & Carmen Cavallaro in "THE TIME, THE PLACE AND THE GIRL" (1946)

THROUGH A THOUSAND DREAMS

Words by
LEO ROBIN

Music by
ARTHUR SCHWARTZ

Once I thought I heard you call-ing from a star.___ Then I caught a glimpse of heav-en from a-far.___ I wait-ed_ and wait-ed_ to find you___ Now, dear one, here we are.___

REFRAIN (*Broadly*)

THROUGH___ A THOU-SAND DREAMS___ My heart___

Love and Learn (1947)

WOULD YOU BELIEVE ME

Lyrics by
CHARLES TOBIAS

Music by
M.K. JEROME and RAY HEINDORF

Escape Me Never (1947)

LOVE FOR LOVE

Lyrics by
TED KOEHLER

Music by
ERICH WOLFGANG KORNGOLD

Performed by Doris Day in "ROMANCE ON THE HIGH SEAS" (1948)

PUT 'EM IN A BOX, TIE 'EM WITH A RIBBON

(And Throw 'Em In The Deep Blue Sea)

Words by
SAMMY CAHN

Music by
JULE STYNE

Performed by Doris Day in "ROMANCE ON THE HIGH SEAS" (1948)

IT'S MAGIC

Words by
SAMMY CAHN

Music by
JULE STYNE

I've heard a-bout Hou-di-ni and the rest of them and I'd put you up a-gainst the best of them,— As far as I'm con-cerned, you're the tops, And you don't — re-sort to props; Things I used to think were in-con-ceiv-a-ble, you've a way of mak-ing them be-liev-a-ble and up-on a night like this I'm a-fraid you just can't miss.

REFRAIN (legato)

You sigh, the song be-gins, You speak and I hear vi-o-lins, IT'S MAG - IC. ____

Performed by Claire Trevor in "KEY LARGO" (1948)

MOANIN' LOW

Words by
HOWARD DIETZ

Music by
RALPH RAINGER

210

It's a Great Feeling (1949)

GIVE ME A SONG WITH A BEAUTIFUL MELODY

Lyrics by
SAMMY CAHN

Music by
JULE STYNE

MELANCHOLY RHAPSODY

Words by
SAMMY CAHN

Music by
RAY HEINDORF

Tune Ukulele

F Bb D G

*Symbols for Guitar and Banjo, Frames for Ukulele

18220-2

215

M.W. & Sons 18220-2

Captain Horatio Hornblower (1951)

LADY BARBARA THEME

By
ROBERT FARNON

Performed by Doris Day in "CALAMITY JANE" (1948)

SECRET LOVE

Words by
PAUL FRANCIS WEBSTER

Music by
SAMMY FAIN

220

I Confess (1953)

LOVE, LOOK WHAT YOU'VE DONE TO ME

Lyrics by
NED WASHINGTON

Music by
DIMITRI TIOMKIN

Days were qui-et and con-tent-ed, nights were peace-ful and se - rene.

Life went a - long like that till love paid a call, and re - ar-ranged the scene.

Love, _____ look what you've done to me, Love, _____ look what you've

So Big (1953)

SELENA'S WALTZ

Music by
MAX STEINER

Meno mosso

The High and the Mighty (1954)

THE HIGH AND THE MIGHTY

Words by
NED WASHINGTON

Music by
DIMITRI TIOMKIN

I was high and might-y, How I laughed at love And the stars a-bove, Then you came like a gen-tle flame And helped me to find my way! I was high and might-y And I told my heart Where to stop and start, Now I find that I was blind, I'm learn-ing it day by day!

225

226

Performed by Judy Garland in "A STAR IS BORN" (1954)

THE MAN THAT GOT AWAY

Words by
IRA GERSHWIN

Music by
HAROLD ARLEN

228

Battle Cry (1955)

HONEY-BABE

Words by
PAUL FRANCIS WEBSTER

Music by
MAX STEINER

Additional Lyrics
HONEY - BABE

3rd Refrain

I don't wanna silver star, honey, honey
I don't wanna silver star, babe, babe;
I don't wanna silver star,
I just wanna candy bar,
Honey, oh baby mine.

(Go to your left, t'ya right, t'ya left)
(Go to your left, t'ya right, t'ya left)

I don't wanna "Rise 'n' shine", honey, honey,
I don't wanna "Rise 'n' shine", babe, babe,
I don't wanna "Rise 'n' shine",
I just wanna sleep 'til nine,
Honey, oh baby mine.

Here we go! Here we go!
On the road that leads to To-ki-o
Doesn't matter where we're from,
Lock the girls up, here we come,
Honey, oh baby mine.

(Go to your left, t'ya right, t'ya left)
(Go to your left, t'ya right, t'ya left)

4th Refrain

Got a gal in ev'ry port, honey, honey
Got a gal in ev'ry port, babe, babe,
Got a gal in ev'ry port,
They're suin' me for non-support,
Honey, oh baby mine.

(Go to your left, t'ya right, t'ya left)
(Go to your left, t'ya right, t'ya left)

Shoo shoo gal in a yellow wig, honey, honey,
Shoo shoo gal in a yellow wig, babe, babe,
Shoo shoo gal in a yellow wig,
I'd dance with her, but her feets too big,
Honey, oh baby mine.

Laura Lee! Laura Lee!
Ain't a dame the same as Laura Lee;
When I whistle, watch her come,
Sticks to me like chewin' gum
Honey, oh baby mine.

(Go to your left, t'ya right, t'ya left)
(Go to your left, t'ya right, t'ya left)

5th Refrain

All we ever do is hike, honey, honey,
All we ever do is hike, babe, babe,
When I get home from this hike,
I'm gonna buy a motor bike,
Honey, oh baby mine.

(Go to your left, t'ya right, t'ya left)
(Go to your left, t'ya right, t'ya left)

Col'nel's ridin' in a jeep, honey, honey,
Col'nel's ridin' in a jeep, babe, babe,
Col'nel's ridin' in a jeep,
But I got blisters on my feet,
Honey, oh baby mine

Look ahead! Look ahead!
When I get back to that feather bed,
Gonna plug up both my ears,
And go to sleep for twenty years!
Honey, oh baby mine.

(Go to your left, t'ya right, t'ya left)
(Go to your left, t'ya right, t'ya left)

6th Refrain

I don't wanna sergeant's stripe, honey, honey,
I don't wanna sergeant's stripe, babe, babe,
'Cause if I had a sergeant's rate,
I wouldn't have no one to hate!
Honey, oh baby mine.

(Go to your left, t'ya right, t'ya left)
(Go to your left, t'ya right, t'ya left)

Nickel in the drink machine, honey, honey,
Nickel in the drink machine, babe, babe,
Down the hatch and never stop,
Gonna drink until I drop,
Honey, oh baby mine.

C'est la guerre! C'est la guerre!
Ain't we livin' like a millionaire?
We get all the food we please,
Powder'd eggs and frozen peas!
Honey, oh baby mine.

(Go to your left, t'ya right, t'ya left)
(Go to your left, t'ya right, t'ya left)

Land of the Pharoahs (1955)

LAND OF THE PHARAOHS

Music by
DIMITRI TIOMKIN

East of Eden (1955)

THEME FROM "EAST OF EDEN"

Music by
LEONARD ROSENMAN

Rebel Without a Cause (1955)

THEME FROM "REBEL WITHOUT A CAUSE"

Music by
LEONARD ROSENMAN

Performed by The Sons Of The Pioneers in "THE SEARCHERS" (1956)

THE SEARCHERS (RIDE AWAY)

Words and Music by
STAN JONES

Giant (1956)

GIANT
(This Then Is Texas)

Words by
PAUL FRANCIS WEBSTER

Music by
DIMITRI TIOMKIN

Rousing March tempo

C Am Dm7 G7

Aus - tin and Hous - ton and A - la - mo, El

C Am Dm7 G7 VERSES C Am F6 G7 C

Pa - so, Crys-tal Cit - y, Wa - co.
Just like a sleep - ing GIANT
My Ma was born in Dal - las,
God made these lone - ly a - cres

C Em F G7 C D7

Sprawl - ing in the sun,
Fath - er in Fort Worth,
Where I ride a - lone
In one great hand the
You can bet your boots I
But the dev - il cursed this

G G9 C F C Am7 D7 Dm7 G7

Ri - o Grande, In the oth - er Gal - ves - ton.
got my roots In the good old Tex - as earth.
land with thirst And he bleached it like a bone.

THEME FROM "HELEN OF TROY"

Music by
MAX STEINER

Moderately

A Face in the Crowd (1957)

A FACE IN THE CROWD

Words by
BUDD SCHULBERG
and **TOM GLAZER**

Music by
TOM GLAZER

THEMES FROM "THE BAD SEED"

By
ALEX NORTH

- 1 -
BERCEUSE

Lyrically - Moderately slow

-2-
LULLABY

-3-
ROMANCE

Moderately

ALEX NORTH

8va bassa

Band of Angels (1957)

BAND OF ANGELS

Words by
CARL SIGMAN

Music by
MAX STEINER

Slowly, with expression

Refrain
sing octave lower

I was a-lone _____ pray-ing for some-one to love, _____ think-ing the moon was a stran-ger. The stars were un-friend-ly and love was a shrine not meant to be mine. I was a-lone _____

Sayonara (1957)

KATSUMI LOVE THEME

Music by
FRANZ WAXMAN

Auntie Mame (1958)

DRIFTING

Words by
KIM GANNON

Music by
BRONISLAU KAPER

THE OLD MAN AND THE SEA

Music by
DIMITRI TIOMKIN

Too Much Too Soon (1958)

TOO MUCH TOO SOON

Words by
AL STILLMAN

Music by
ERNEST GOLD

THEME FROM A SUMMER PLACE

Words by
MACK DISCANT

Music by
MAX STEINER

265

Performed by Gene Kelly in "MARJORIE MORNINGSTAR" (1958)

A VERY PRECIOUS LOVE

Words by
PAUL FRANCIS WEBSTER

Music by
SAMMY FAIN

REFRAIN *(Tenderly with much expression)*

Performed by Frank Sinatra in "ROBIN AND THE SEVEN HOODS" (1964)

MY KIND OF TOWN (Chicago Is)

Words by
SAMMY CAHN

Music by
JAMES VAN HEUSEN

270

271

273

THEME FROM THE SUNDOWNERS

By
DIMITRI TIOMKIN

Moderately slow

The Dark at the Top of the Stairs (1960)

THEME FROM "THE DARK AT THE TOP OF THE STAIRS"

Music by
MAX STEINER

Parrish (1961)

LUCY'S THEME

Music by
MAX STEINER

Performed by Emilio Pericoli in "ROME ADVENTURE" (1962)

AL DI LA

**English Words by
ERVIN DRAKE
Original Italian Words by
MOGOL**

**Music by
C. DONIDA**

Splendor in the Grass (1961)

THEME FROM "SPLENDOR IN THE GRASS"

By
DAVID AMRAM

Slowly with much expression

The Chapman Report (1962)

THEME FROM THE CHAPMAN REPORT

By
LEONARD ROSENMAN

DAYS OF WINE AND ROSES

Words by
JOHNNY MERCER

Music by
HENRY MANCINI

THE THEME FROM AMERICA AMERICA

Greek Lyric by
NIKOS GATSOS

Music by
MANOS HADJIDAKIS

Cheyenne Autumn (1964)

AUTUMN'S BALLAD

Music by
ALEX NORTH

Performed by Natalie Wood in "INSIDE DAISY CLOVER" (1965)

YOU'RE GONNA HEAR FROM ME

Words by
DORY PREVIN

Music by
ANDRE' PREVIN

293

An American Dream (1966)

A TIME FOR LOVE
From "An American Dream"

Words by
PAUL FRANCIS WEBSTER

Music by
JOHNNY MANDEL

Harper (1966)

SURE AS YOU'RE BORN

Lyrics by
MARILYN and ALAN BERGMAN

Music by
JOHNNY MANDEL

299

WAIT UNTIL DARK

Words by
JAY LIVINGSTON and RAY EVANS

Music by
HENRY MANCINI

Performed by Carmen McRae in "HOTEL" (1967)

THIS HOTEL

Lyrics by
RICHARD QUINE

Music by
JOHNNY KEATING

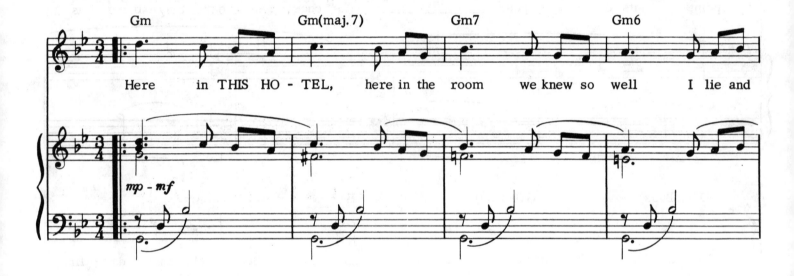

Here in THIS HO-TEL, here in the room we knew so well I lie and

stare now; _____ Here where love was born, my eyes are

Petulia (1968)

PETULIA

Words by
CAROLYN LEIGH

Music by
JOHN BARRY

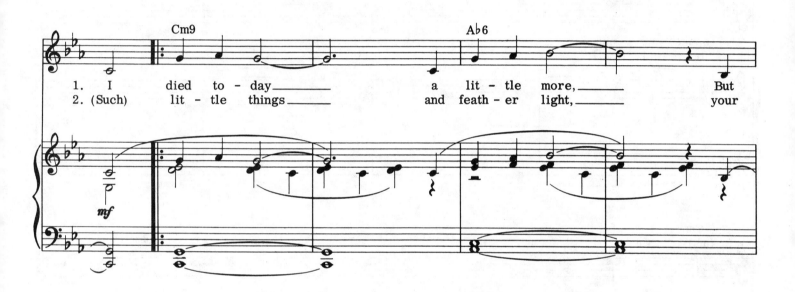

1. I died to - day_____ a lit - tle more,_____ But
2. (Such) lit - tle things_____ and feath - er light,_____ your

noth - ing's lost,_____ I've died be - fore;_____ I
hand in mine,_____ the sum - mer night;_____ Such

308

The Fox (1968)

THEME FROM "THE FOX"

By
LALO SCHIFRIN

Moderately slow

311

THE HEART IS A LONELY HUNTER

Lyrics by
PEGGY LEE

Music by
DAVID GRUSIN

314

Picasso Summer (1969)

SUMMER ME, WINTER ME

Lyrics by
MARILYN and ALAN BERGMAN

Music by
MICHEL LEGRAND

Summer of '42 (1971)

THE SUMMER KNOWS
(Theme from "SUMMER OF 42")

Words by
MARILYN and ALAN BERGMAN

Music by
MICHEL LEGRAND

Performed by Maureen McGovern in "THE TOWERING INFERNO" (1974)

WE MAY NEVER LOVE LIKE THIS AGAIN

Words and Music by
AL KASHA and JOEL HIRSCHHORN

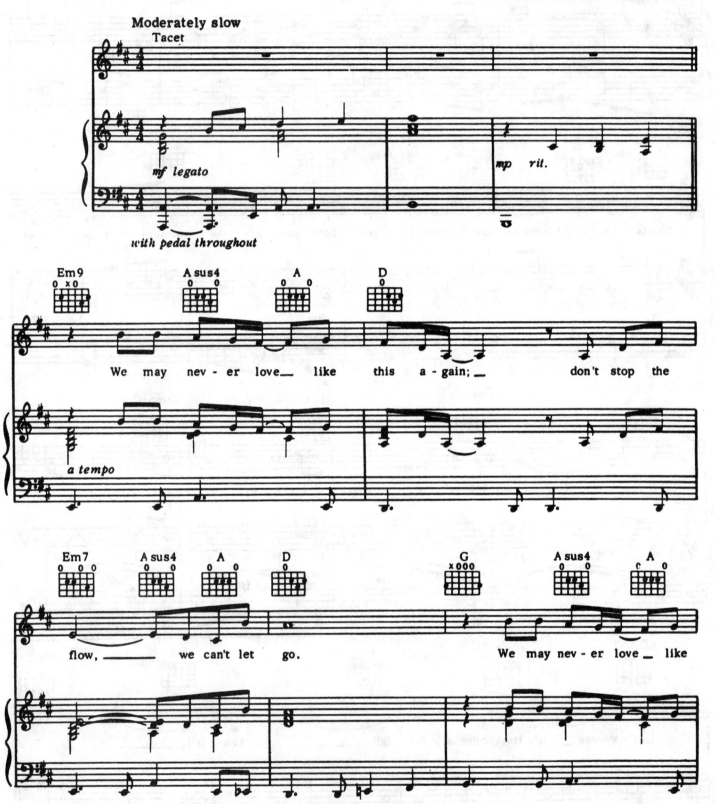

321

Performed by Margot Kidder in "SUPERMAN" (1978)

CAN YOU READ MY MIND?

Words by
LESLIE BRICUSSE

Music by
JOHN WILLIAMS

Performed by Barbra Streisand in "A STAR IS BORN" (1976)

EVERGREEN

(LOVE THEME FROM "A STAR IS BORN")

Words by
PAUL WILLIAMS

MUSIC BY
BARBRA STREISAND

Superman (1978)

THEME FROM "SUPERMAN"

By
JOHN WILLIAMS

SONG FROM "10"

(IT'S EASY TO SAY)

Lyric by
ROBERT WELLS

Music by
HENRY MANCINI

Performed by Rod Stewart in "NIGHT SHIFT" (1982)

THAT'S WHAT FRIENDS ARE FOR

Words and Music by
BURT BACHARACH and
CAROLE BAYER SAGER

Repeat and fade
Vocal ad lib.

CHARIOTS OF FIRE

By
VANGELIS

343

Performed by James Ingram & Patti Austin in "BEST FRIENDS" (1982)

HOW DO YOU KEEP THE MUSIC PLAYING?

Music by
MICHEL LEGRAND

Words by
ALAN and MARILYN BERGMAN

346

Performed by Christopher Cross in "ARTHUR" (1981)

ARTHUR'S THEME

(BEST THAT YOU CAN DO)

Words and Music by
BURT BACHARACH,
CAROLE BAYER SAGER
CHRISTOPHER CROSS and PETER ALLEN

Once in your life, you'll find __
Ar - thur, he does what he

Driving Miss Daisy (1989)

DRIVING MISS DAISY

Music by
HANS ZIMMER
Arranged by Shirley Walker

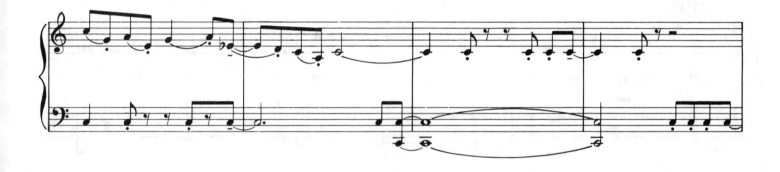

The Accidental Tourist (1988)

THEME FROM "THE ACCIDENTAL TOURIST"

Music by
JOHN WILLIAMS

Batman (1989)

THE BATMAN THEME

Music Composed by
DANNY ELFMAN

Curly Sue (1991)

YOU NEVER KNOW

Words and Music by
JOHN BETTIS and STEVE DORFF

You nev-er see ex-act-ly where the road will lead you. And when it comes to love, you

gam-ble when you need to. You'll may-be break your heart on one un-luck-y throw

but then a-gain you nev-er know.

know.

but then a - gain you nev - er

Repeat and fade (Instrumental)

know,

Performed by Bryan Adams in "ROBIN HOOD, PRINCE OF THIEVES" (1991)

(EVERYTHING I DO) I DO IT FOR YOU

Written by
BRYAN ADAMS, ROBERT JOHN LANGE
and MICHAEL KAMEN

369

JFK (1991)

THEME FROM "JFK"

Music by
JOHN WILLIAMS

Unforgiven (1992)

CLAUDIA'S THEME

Music by
CLINT EASTWOOD

Moderately, with expression

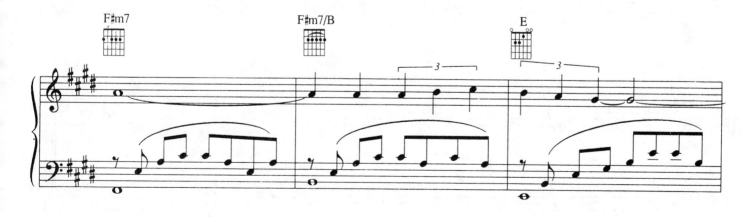

377

Performed by Antonio Banderas in "THE MAMBO KINGS" (1992)

BEAUTIFUL MARIA OF MY SOUL

(Bella Maria De Mi Alma")

Lyrics by
ARNE GLIMCHER

Music by
ROBERT KRAFT

Beau - ti - ful Mar - i - a of my soul,

oh, oh, oh.

(Trumpet Solo)

D.C. al Coda

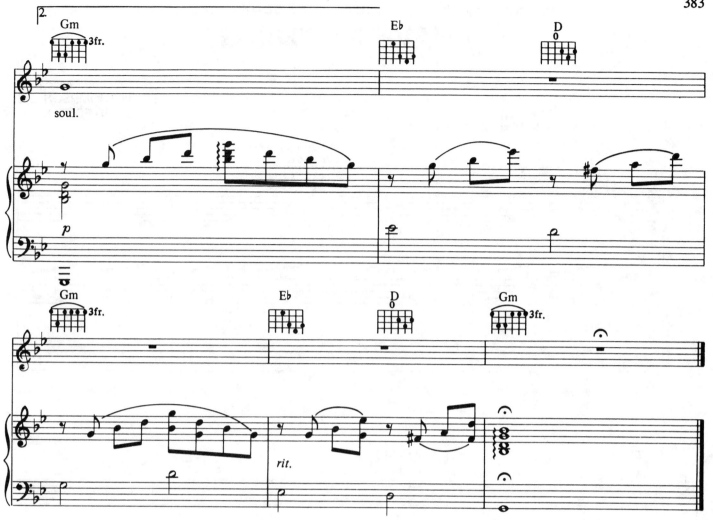

soul.

Si deseo sonreir	En un caracol
Pienso solamente en ti	Pienso oir tu voz
En la magia de tu amor	La bella Maria de mi amor
En tu piel, en tu sabor	
	Aunque esternos separados
En la isla del dolor	En un sueno angelicar
Recuerdo tu calor	Si llego de nuevo amar
Desearia morir	No hay razon, porque cambiar
Cerca de ti	
	Temo yo permancer
Un ardiente corazon	Sin ti en la eternidad
Colorea mi pasion	Lejos nos puedon separar
Deseando compartir	Jamas pudiera olvidar
El sentir de este vivir	Tu risa celestial
	Tus besos, tu calor
En las olas de este mar	La bella Maria de mi amor
Sueno en la eternidad	
Con cada luna vendras	Si no te vuelva a ver
Con la merea te iras	No dejaras de ser
	La bella Maria de mi amor

Performed by Whitney Houston in "THE BODYGUARD" (1992)

I HAVE NOTHING

Words and Music by
LINDA THOMPSON and
DAVID FOSTER

Moderately, with "2" feel

Pedal throughout

Share my life, take me for what I am. 'Cause
You see through, right to the heart of me. You

I CROSS MY HEART

Words and Music by
STEVE DORFF and ERIC KAZ

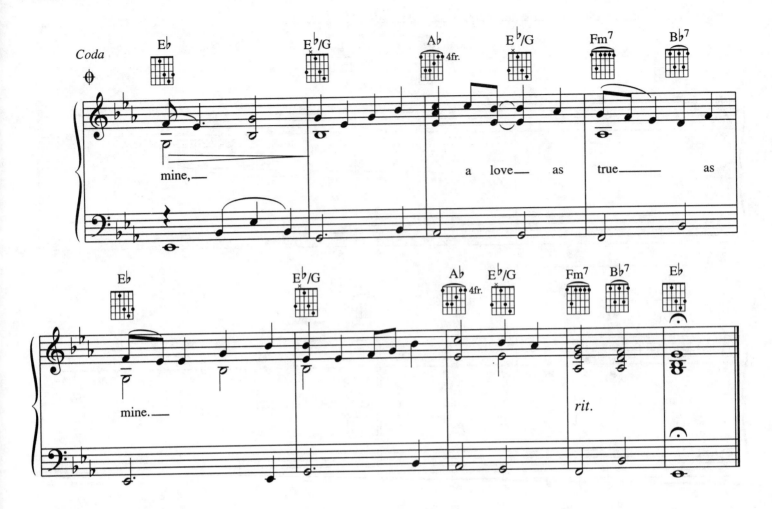

Additional Lyrics

2. You will always be the miracle
   That makes my life complete.
   And as long as there's a breath in me
   I'll make yours just as sweet.
   As we look into the future,
   It's as far as we can see.
   So let's make each tomorrow
   Be the best that it can be.
   (To Chorus)

Free Willy (1993)

FREE WILLY
(Main Title Theme)

Music by
BASIL POLEDOURIS

401

Performed by Michael Jackson on the soundtrack of "FREE WILLY" (1993)

WILL YOU BE THERE

Written and Composed by
MICHAEL JACKSON

Hold me___ like the Riv - er Jor - dan,___ and I will then
wear - y, ___ tell me will you hold me,___ when wrong, will you

say to thee___ you are my friend.___ me? But they
scold me,___ when lost will you find me? But they

Car - ry me,___ like you are my broth - er.___ Love me like a
told me___ a man should be faith - ful___ and walk when not

Dennis the Menace (1987)

DENNIS THE MENACE
(Main Title Theme)

Music by
JERRY GOLDSMITH

Moderately fast

MAIN TITLE FROM "THE FUGITIVE"

Music by
JAMES NEWTON HOWARD

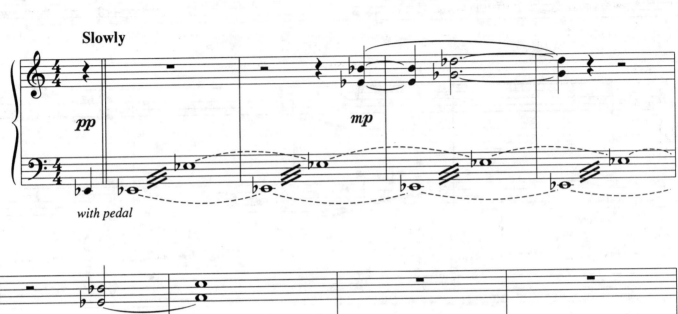

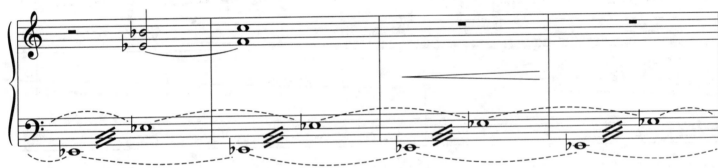

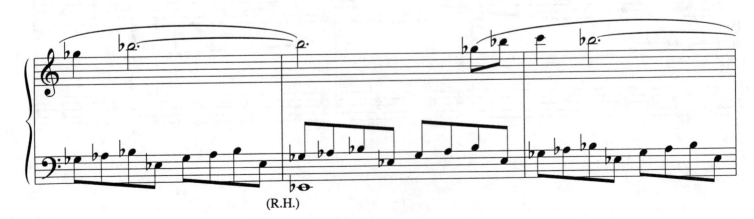